THE CHRISTIAN INSTITUTE

The Christian Origins of Humanism

REVD DR RICHARD TURNBULL

Copyright © The Christian Institute 2023

The author has asserted his right under Section 77 of the Copyright, Designs & Patents Act 1988 to be identified as the author of this work.

Printed in April 2023

ISBN 978-1-901086-56-0

Published by:
The Christian Institute, Wilberforce House, 4 Park Road, Gosforth Business Park, Newcastle upon Tyne, NE12 8DG

All rights reserved

No part of this publication may be reproduced, or stored in a retrieval system, or transmitted, in any form or by any means, mechanical, electronic, photocopying, recording or otherwise, without the prior permission of The Christian Institute.

All scripture quotations, unless otherwise indicated, are taken from the HOLY BIBLE, NEW INTERNATIONAL VERSION®. NIV®. Copyright © 1973, 1978, 1984 by International Bible Society. Used by permission of Zondervan. All rights reserved.

The Christian Institute is a Company Limited by Guarantee, registered in England as a charity. Company No. 263 4440, Charity No. 100 4774. A charity registered in Scotland. Charity No. SC039220

Contents

5	Foreword
6	The Origins of Humanism
8	Definitions and meanings
12	Key features and characteristics
17	Influence on the Reformers
20	Erasmus: Prince of Humanists (1466-1536)
22	Erasmus of Rotterdam: key elements of life
25	Erasmus of Rotterdam: significant works
29	Erasmus' Greek edition of the New Testament
33	Conclusion and evaluation

Foreword

We have come to think of humanism as something to oppose. Secular humanism represents what most Christians view as the advance of the secular state: policy proposals and decisions which are based upon the centrality and priority of human reason or rationality without reference to God at all, never mind any basis in the revelation given in Holy Scripture.

Perhaps advocates of the secular agenda and modern-day humanism might be surprised to learn that the origins of humanism are deeply Christian and that the ideas profoundly influenced many of the Reformers. We can see in the history of humanism enormous strengths which we can recover for the benefit of the Christian faith in the public square, whilst also recognising some characteristics which later developed into what we might indeed call secular, rationalistic, human-centred humanism. Originally, humanism was an expression of human flourishing *under* God, not *apart* from him. The ideas of humanism were foundational for the translation, accuracy and availability of the Scriptures in languages we could understand. We should not surrender the idea of human flourishing to the secular humanists; our belief is that such flourishing derives from our relationship with God.

The Origins of Humanism

Medieval Catholicism was built on several pillars which held up a system not only of corrupt piety, but also of theological error. Two of these pillars were, first, the idea and authority of the Papacy and, secondly, the nature of the 'mass', the Lord's Supper. Humanism very effectively undermined both of these impediments to scriptural beliefs. We should seek to understand why.

The Papacy, at least in part, based its claim to power and authority on a document, *The Donation of Constantine*, which claimed to be a grant to the Pope of sweeping powers throughout the Christian world by the fourth century convert, the Emperor, Constantine I. This supposed endowment functioned as a central plank of the papal claim to a universal temporal jurisdiction.

There had always been some doubt around the veracity of the document but by the time of the fifteenth century several scholars using new, humanist techniques of analysis were challenging the authenticity of this document anew.

Prime amongst these was an early humanist scholar who worked in the Vatican, Lorenzo Valla (1407-1457). Few, today, have ever heard of him. Yet, in 1440, Valla, using textual and linguistic analysis, demolished the claims of the *Donation* and effectively proved it to be a forgery from the eighth century thus destabilising in an instant one of the central props of papal authority.[1]

Subsequently, not least with the publication of a new Greek edition of the New Testament in 1516, to which we shall come, the priority given to original sources and texts exposed much of the piety of medieval Catholicism (purgatory, relics, the mass) to more rigorous translations of the Scriptures and, unsurprisingly, many of those beliefs and practices were found wanting. However, here also lies the central tension of the original humanism. What we find is an approach, a method, which gave weight to original sources and texts and a priority to textual analysis which exposed much of the fabric of the medieval Catholic church. In that sense, humanism was a reforming movement.

Indeed, these methods and approaches were all adopted by the Reformers, many of whom, Zwingli, Calvin, Melanchthon, were deeply influenced by humanism. The question, however, is the extent to which the humanists were primarily reformers (lower case) due to their scholarly methods compared to the Reformers were primarily Reformers (upper case) due to the content of their thought. Humanism in the sense of techniques and approaches did not change but became allied at the Reformation to a renewal of Augustinian theology and spirituality.

Definitions and meanings

Humanism is a complex and rather difficult phenomenon to define. Partially this is due to the fact that the term has not been used in its original fifteenth and sixteenth century contexts. Instead, it was a rather nebulous movement which scholars subsequently labelled 'humanism'. The word as describing the Renaissance was invented by German Lutheran scholar F. I Niethhammer (1766-1848). He did not intend it in an anti-Christian sense but merely as summing up the concerns of Renaissance thinking. Since then, the term 'humanist' has come to mean someone who rejects the claims of revealed faith. This was certainly not the case with the first humanists, the vast majority of whom were patently sincere Christians (though with varying degrees of devotion) who wished to apply their learning and enthusiasm to the exploration and proclamation, and indeed reform, of the Christian faith.

Yet there is no doubt that by the beginning of the sixteenth century there was a well-established transnational movement with a strong sense of identity, albeit with a range of emphases and diversity. This movement was essential to the course of the Reformation. At its most basic level the term 'humanism' referred to the centrality and flourishing of the human person under God, not the rationalistic denial of God.

Humanism essentially meant the study of what we would call today the literature of the humanities, the recovery of emphasis on the classical sources of both Pagan and Christian antiquity, thus opening up new avenues and vistas of inquiry in history, literature and theology. Any attempt to impose the modern secular definitions upon Renaissance humanism must be resisted.

Alister McGrath in *The Intellectual Origins of the European Reformation*[2] sets out four alternative views of humanism, which helps explain some of the diversity.

- First, Renaissance humanism as *the birth of modern consciousness*. This idea was exemplified in the writings of the nineteenth-century Swiss historian, Jacob Burckhardt; humanism in this outlook does indeed prepare the ground for the embrace of individualism, secularism and moral autonomy that characterised the Enlightenment. One can see where the modern definitions of humanism come from if we embrace this approach to definition.
- Secondly, an almost polar opposite point of view, expounded by Giuseppe Tofannin, a twentieth century Italian writer who in 1954 wrote a *History of Humanism*. This point of view sees the Italian humanists, in particular, as *exponents of an authentically Christian culture* in the face of the onslaught and challenge of both heterodoxy and paganism. In this instance there is no debate; humanism brings the Christian origins of our culture, literature, politics, law and so on to the forefront of public debate.
- Thirdly, *civic humanism*, a term introduced in 1928 by the German-American historian of political thought and literature, Hans Baron. This was essentially a view that humanism was primarily concerned with government and that the best form of government was, based on studies of the classic republicanism of ancient Rome and Greece, derived from the moral and political insights of republicanism. Florence was seen as an example, as was a new appreciation of Cicero, the great Roman statesman and philosopher. However, McGrath points out that the Florentine humanism of the medieval period did not seem overly concerned with republicanism, more with rhetoric, a feature we will return to subsequently. Nevertheless, we have the category of *civic humanism*.
- Fourthly, a view endorsed by McGrath, which sees

humanism as 'essentially cultural and educational, primarily concerned with written and spoken eloquence, and only secondarily concerned with matters of philosophy and politics'[3] – or indeed doctrine. A weakness of this approach, indeed a weakness of the humanist exercise, to which point we will also return, is its failure to see the latter as primary. This is humanism as a *method*.

What these different approaches reveal is the remarkable diversity which characterised Renaissance humanism, and whereas we can see the beginnings of trends which led, ultimately, in the direction of modern enlightenment, rationalistic, secular humanism, those features did not lie at the heart of the original movement. There are some distinctions to be drawn between humanists in different parts of Europe. Erasmus represented a more global view, regarding national boundaries and languages as impediments; the Swiss humanists a more nationalistic expression of humanism of which Zwingli was unquestionably a part. However, we can also see how some combination of McGrath's second and fourth definitions give a strong basis of seeing humanism as the *flourishing of the human person under God, giving expression to an authentically Christian expression in the public square, built upon the appropriation of original sources and texts, primarily in the Scriptures.*

Humanists then saw themselves primarily as 'men of letters', concerned with language, text and written and spoken eloquence. Their influence was unquestionably an elitist one and ranged from high scholarship and influential patrons to colleges and academies pouring over Greek and Latin grammars. As MacCulloch says, "Humanists were lovers and connoisseurs of words."[4] Hence words contained power to change the world. These words, which inspired such excitement, were found in ancient texts from long-vanished societies with the same belief in the transforming power of poetry, oratory and rhetoric – ancient Greece and Rome. Humanism brought about a new emphasis and respect on those parts of the curriculum seen as secondary by the medieval scholastics. The objective was to get as clear a picture as possible of ancient societies (so to model the best today for the common good) and to obtain the highest quality possible versions of ancient texts (so that we might have the most genuine picture). The humanist sense of the past also alerted scholars to the problem of anachronism and thus enabled them to detect spurious and forged documents – taking us back to Valla and the *Donation of Constantine*. This concern for accuracy and genuineness of the text, also exposed and brought into the light, as we will see, textual inaccuracies with direct relevance for the accuracy of the biblical text and indeed for Reformation theology. We will see this particularly when we consider Erasmus' production of the New Testament in Greek; the epitome of the humanist project and a central enabling feature for the Reformation. These emphases then became vehicles for reform, reform not least of the medieval church. The methods and approaches also became central tools in the armoury of the Protestant Reformers. Again, as MacCulloch argues:

> *Ad fontes*, back to the sources, was the battle-cry of the humanists, and Protestants would take it over from them.[5]

We can almost feel the tension between form and content as, at least in part, explaining both the attraction of humanism to the Reformers and also its limitations. It is, however, to these key features that we will now turn.

Key features and characteristics

What then were the key features and characteristics of humanism?

1. Reaction against scholasticism
Scholasticism is the name given to the theologians and theological method of the medieval period. Obscurity of the text rather than its clarity might be the watch word. The concern was with a carefully structured argument and a philosophical approach to the text. This methodology dominated the universities of the medieval era. The scholastic method was dialectic; establish a proposition and then set up arguments for and against; a method we see in Peter Lombard's *Sentences*, one of the classic scholastic texts. The text as such often seemed secondary to the argument. The humanist approach, however, was through the text itself, language and rhetoric. To the humanists, the scholastics were overly concerned with abstract ideas, dislocated from actual historical context, rather than lived experience. As Timothy George put it, humanists saw scholasticism as "arid speculations which led to an intellectual labyrinth".[6] Humanists sneered at what they considered the barbarous style of the scholastic method; they viewed the method as not only pointlessly speculative, but also wildly irrelevant to everyday life.

Humanists often avoided posts in universities (though probably less so as time went on) preferring independent sponsorship. Hence, they would often portray themselves as men of ideas closely involved with ordinary life and the business of government and society rather than isolated ivory-tower academics who wasted their time arguing about how many angels could dance on the head of a pin – although this is a famous caricature of scholasticism portrayed by humanists.

Humanists and Reformers often found themselves attacking the same old scholastic theologians. So Erasmus in his *Praise of Folly*:

> Then there are the theologians, a remarkably supercilious and touchy lot...They interpret hidden mysteries to suit themselves: how the world was created and designed; through what channels the stain of sin filtered down to posterity; by what means, in what measure, and how long Christ was formed in the Virgin's womb; how, in the Eucharist, accidents can subsist without a domicile. But this sort of question has been discussed threadbare.[7]

Even in style the differences from the old scholasticism were clearly observed. The scholastic text would be in a Gothic style which was intended to look more 'hand-written.' Humanist scholars sought precision and clarity in copying ancient manuscripts; their printers followed suit with typefaces much closer to what we are used to today. Similarly, in architecture and the wider arts, buildings, sculpture, paintings and gardens were more and more accurately imitated from the sources of ancient Greece and Rome.

Humanists used their methods to attack corruption and superstition in the church, ranging from their reaction to the mystical and magical, the cult of saints, relics and other corrupt pietistic practices. This is a further example of how humanism allied with the Reformation.

2. *The quest for and priority of original sources*
The new humanism of the Renaissance led to a flood of manuscripts, their distribution and a new emphasis on ancient languages in order to be able to read the newly discovered reservoir of texts. Medieval Europe had remarkably little access to Greek texts, and hence little knowledge of the Greek language. Both of these were corrected in the advent of humanism. The hunt for original texts relating to ancient societies led to a flood of discoveries; and to understand the Greek, the language must be learnt. We will see subsequently how this led to Erasmus' new edition of the Greek New Testament, which

was foundational for Reformation theology. However, we can see how this project began to emerge, with the cry of – *ad fontes* – 'to the sources'. In addition, the introduction of paper and the advent of the printing press meant that these texts, and their translations, could be accurately reproduced, and then widely circulated. The great humanist centres were often also the eminent commercial centres, bringing scholarship and printing together in places which could accumulate and mobilise the huge capital needed to finance the mass production of books; scholarship, printing, commerce – yet another link of humanism and the Reformation.

3. The nature and priority of the text
How might one establish authenticity amid, what MacCulloch refers to as, "this intoxicating but unsorted flow of information?"[8] One aspect was to assess the text in every possible way:
- content
- dating
- origins
- motives
- appearance
- clarity

Consequently, a great deal depended on texts being accurate. This meant that humanist methodology had to develop ways of distinguishing a good, accurate text from a corrupt or forged text. This was indeed a new approach:

> In earlier centuries, monks cheerfully forged documents on a huge scale for the greater glory of God, particularly charters proving their monastery's claim to lands or privileges.[9]

It was this quest that led to the clarion call of *ad fontes*, back to the sources, for it was in the original sources, in their original languages, in an accurate text that authenticity would be found. This also meant a new emphasis on translation and the principles of translation. We can easily see the importance for biblical studies. And for the Reformers, of course, it was not just authenticity which was found, but truth. This authentic truth could, and would, stand against even the greatest authority of the medieval church: the Papacy itself.

The humanist emphasis on authentic text also challenged the classic scholastic method of glosses and commentaries which were to be by-passed in favour of engagement with the text itself. We will see this when we look at the translation of the Bible in more detail. However, the humanist approach to the text was, generally, to consider the text as an organised whole rather than simply an assembly of information. The effect on the Reformation is shown by Philip Melanchthon's commentary on Romans in 1519 presenting Paul's epistle as an organised account of justification by faith, superbly combining evangelical theology and humanist rhetorical analysis. The emphasis on text did sit more easily with the Protestant principle of *sola scriptura* than the weight given to tradition in Catholicism.

4. *Rhetoric and language*

Rhetoric, described by Richard Rex as "queen among the arts of Renaissance humanism",[10] was also of particular importance for Christian scholars, most manifestly in the art of preaching. Humanism was intended to produce orators, those skilled in the art of rhetoric which equipped them to debate and persuade. Cicero, of course, was a master of rhetoric. Now, with regard to preaching, it is clearly not the case that the medieval church did not believe or practice preaching. The official title of the Dominican order is 'the Order of Preachers'. There are numerous preaching manuals and manuscript sermons deriving from the medieval period. As Rex comments:

> The church did not need humanists to tell it of the importance of preaching. But, given the enormous interest in preaching, it is hardly surprising that the techniques of classical rhetoric,

recovered by the humanists, were soon applied in this field.[11]

However, much of this preaching became triumphalist and complacent; the Reformers rather reacted against this. The study of rhetoric also affected reading as well as writing, which takes us back again to the humanist concern with texts. Humanism substituted rhetoric for dialectic. Zwingli employed humanist rhetorical techniques in his debate with Luther over the eucharist by deploying the methodology of the figure of speech to texts such as 'this is my body'. Humanist method did affect Reformation practice and Reformation doctrine.

Influence on the Reformers

So, let's turn to an assessment of where we are in our discussion of the place of humanism. We start with Alister McGrath's summary:

> Both humanist and Reformer has serious misgivings concerning scholastic theology; both wished to return to the Bible, particularly the New Testament, as the source of Christian doctrine; both greatly valued the [early church] fathers as witnesses to the vitality and character of early Christianity. This appeared to indicate that both movements possessed a common theological program...[12]

Indeed, it was humanist scholars who projected the dispute which Martin Luther had generated in the theology faculty at Wittenburg, not least by his attack on indulgences in the Ninety-Five Theses, into such a major controversy within the church globally with all of the ramifications for the course of the Reformation. However, to what extent were the leading Reformers influenced by humanism and what, if any, were the areas of difference?

Zwingli (1484-1531) was clearly very significantly influenced by humanism. This is reflected in his early sermons and preaching at Zurich, and yet, from 1520, Zwingli, with the city council, adopted the principle of *sola scriptura* as the basis for preaching and authority which clearly established him as Reformer rather than humanist. Zwingli had come under humanist influence at the University of Vienna from 1498 and Swiss humanism carried with it strongly nationalistic overtones; Zwingli died on the battlefield in defence of his native city. The location of Switzerland was conducive to contact and movement between northern and southern Europe; printing presses were established in the major Swiss cities and humanist scholars promoted the renewal of life, structure and vitality of the church, if not doctrine. Zwingli adopted humanist method to argue for the right of clergy to marry and the reception of communion in both kinds. Zwingli's personal library contained the works of Erasmus, as well as Luther, the former, according to McGrath, heavily annotated.[13] Zwingli visited Erasmus in Basel in 1516 shortly after the latter's publication of a Greek text of the New Testament. Zwingli clearly applied humanist method to Scripture but drew more precise doctrinal conclusions rather than merely celebrating the eloquence. Zwingli also gave greater weight to a pessimistic human anthropology and to the doctrine of divine providence; though he also appealed to the philosopher Seneca as well as Scripture in support.

Calvin (1509-1564) was also influenced. For Calvin, as a second-generation reformer, there is little doubt about the early humanist influence. His first publication was a commentary on a work of Seneca. Even later, Calvin's technique reflects humanist method. His approach to scriptural interpretation was clarity and brevity. It is also clear, of course, that Calvin, at some point in the early 1530s, moved to a more explicit Reformation position. The debate in Calvin over natural theology also illustrates both the continuity and discontinuity. Calvin engages with and adopts much of the outlook of Cicero in the 1559 edition of the *Institutes* until he discussed the inadequacy of natural revelation where Calvin asserts the true knowledge of God comes from Scripture alone. This debate, however, has occupied Calvin scholars ever since.

So influences, yes, but there are also profound differences. For the Reformers, particularly Luther, the scholastics were not, per se, to be criticised on account of their style of vocabulary, but on account of their theology. Alister McGrath says:

> A reformation of doctrine, rather than of style or vocabulary, was the real issue at stake.[14]

Timothy George also notes:

> Despite the significance of humanism as a preparation for the Reformation, most of the humanists, Erasmus chief among them, never attained either the sense of gravity of the human condition or of the triumph of divine grace which marked the theology of the Reformers. Humanism, like mysticism, was part of the scaffolding which enabled the reformers to question certain assumptions of the received tradition, but which in itself was not sufficient to provide an enduring response to the haunting questions of the age.[15]

Humanism began and ended as a technique. The humanist emphasis on education, rhetoric, dialogue, criticism, reform and ethics was all well and good but the Reformation weight given to human depravity, the sovereignty of grace and the importance of doctrine rather overshadowed the mild, moderate and moralistic optimism of humanism. Without humanism there may not have been a Reformation as we know it; yet they are not equal partners; the Reformation went significantly further than humanism would allow, not least in the nature and understanding of Scripture and doctrine.

Erasmus: Prince of Humanists (1466-1536)

Certainly in Reformation studies the mention of humanism immediately conjours up the image of Erasmus of Rotterdam. Laurel Carrington, writing in Carter Lindberg's book, *The Reformation Theologians*, describes Erasmus in these terms:

> Recognized as the prince of humanists, the leading biblical scholar of his age, and a powerful advocate of church reform, he nevertheless came under devastating attack from both the Catholic theologians of Louvain and Paris and the adherents to Luther's evangelical reform.[16]

Who was Erasmus? He was committed to spiritual renewal and reform, his humanist approach to text was a lynchpin of Luther's Reformation and his *Novum Testamentum* was a tour de force of epoch-making significance. Yet, he remained a Roman Catholic throughout his life and never threw his lot in with the doctrinal as well as spiritual aspects of the Reformation. Nevertheless, to Catholic critics at the time, it was said that 'Erasmus laid the egg, and Luther hatched it', indeed a common examination question in undergraduate Reformation studies today. In other words, he laid the groundwork.

We do not find in Erasmus a systematic exposition of theology. However, he formulated a theological curriculum, as well as edited, translated, paraphrased and expouded biblical and patristic texts. He commented on doctrinal questions and offered spiritual advice in devotional tracts. He wrote a number of crucially important works, some of which we will consider.

As a humanist, biblical scholar and reformer, Erasmus

emphasised the primacy of language both in understanding God's communication to humanity and indeed in our response. Thus he emphasised inner spiritual renewal and piety over doctrinal formulations and gave more weight to inner convictions over outward ceremonies – which led him into much criticism of the industry of piety which dominated the medieval church. He also emphasised the role of the word as mediator between God and the believer. Hence we find the enigma of Erasmus: a great mind, a great reformer, foundational to the Reformation, the translator of the New Testament, and yet, in another sense, not a Reformer!

Erasmus of Rotterdam: key elements of life

Erasmus was born in 1467 in Gouda, near Rotterdam in the Netherlands, the illegitimate son of a priest, a situation sadly not uncommon at the time. His baptismal name was Erasmus, he later added, 'of Rotterdam' and the other name by which he is known, Desiderius, was a later literary addition. We don't know very much about his youth and upbringing; Erasmus himself sought to draw a veil over what he regarded as a stain and embarrassment. He was educated in Gouda and in Deventer, in the rural Netherlands, under the brothers of the Brethren of the Common Life. In 1487, Erasmus joined the Augustinian order of canons regular at Steyn, a monastery near Gouda. The biographer of Erasmus, Cornelius Augustijn, comments that "the first thirty years of his life show no sign of any special talent".[17]

In his later life Erasmus claimed that he had been placed in the monastery against his will and he complained bitterly about the burdens of monastic life. He certainly made good use of the monastery library, improving his own writing and even encountering some humanist scholarship. In 1493, Erasmus left the monastery to become secretary to the Bishop of Cambrai; then in 1495 to study theology in Paris. He was never to return to the order, despite an instruction to do so in 1514. By 1507, Erasmus had abandoned the traditional monastic habit, his future trajectory now clear. In his theological studies in Paris we know that he was introduced to scholastic theology. His view is made quite clear by Augustijn, quoting in part from a letter of Erasmus:

> ...the lectures were hair-splitting, sophistical quibbling, which made men into quarrelsome pseudo-scholars, one

dispute followed another, all quarrels about nothing, and "we sometimes debate questions of a sort intolerable to truly religious men."[18]

Erasmus' time in Paris exposed him to the rigours of scholasticism, which he thoroughly disliked. It also proved an opportunity for him to expand his contacts within the world of letters he so eagerly desired to join, and to begin to get his own writing into circulation. He never completed his doctoral work at Paris but was later awarded a doctorate in theology from the University of Turin. In 1499, he travelled to England with the help of a new patron, Lord Mountjoy encountered Thomas More and the humanist scholar, later Dean of St Paul's, John Colet, hearing the latter's lectures on Paul's epistles. From this point on, Erasmus turned his interest in literature to biblical scholarship, which became his lifelong pursuit. In the coming years he travelled in England, Paris, Orleans, Netherlands and Italy. After 1504 he did not live in the Netherlands again. During many of these years and sojourns in different places the mere struggle to exist took much of his energy. He did not break free from his dependency on others until his mid-forties. He survived by a combination of gifts and income from supervising pupils. Stephen Gardiner, later Bishop of Winchester and persecutor of Protestant reformers, cooked for Erasmus in Paris in 1511 as a boy of 15-years old. What Gardiner later recalled was the books, Greek and Latin, which Erasmus buried himself under.

Erasmus had grown into and emerged as a Christian humanist. He was drawn to the pagan literature of ancient Greece and Rome, which he believed was an essential component of the development of a well-formed mind. As a Christian humanist, Erasmus worked to draw together both pagan and Christian sources to effect a transformation of the spirit through language. He regarded the language of Scripture as paramount, yet the pagan classics also served a purpose as well. Through mastery of the good literature of the past Christians could learn how to love both what is morally good and the truth that Christ had prepared for them, something they would never be inspired to do through reading the crabbed and distorted Latin of the scholastic theologians.

Erasmus of Rotterdam: significant works

Erasmus published a wide range of publications and materials which, inevitably, to some degree reflect the different periods of his life. However, it is possible to establish his main works and summarise his views which then demonstrate to us both the continuities and discontinuities with the wider reformers. Erasmus' major works can be summarised as follows:

- Enchiridion Militis Christiani (1501) – Handbook of the Christian Soldier
- Praise of Folly (1509)
- Colloquies (1518)
- Novum Testamentum (1516)

Let's have a look at the first two of these.

1. Enchiridion Militis Christiani

Erasmus wrote this in 1501 at the request of the wife of a soldier, the master of arms at the court of Burgundy, to win him away from his all too rough life. The book was not really very successful at first despite several editions. In 1518 Erasmus had the book printed in Basel with the content unchanged but with a new foreword in which he unmistakably took Luther under his protection against his enemies.

The *Enchiridion* has as its point of departure the idea that life is a struggle against the demons and the world. In this struggle, God gives us two weapons, prayer and knowledge, which we acquire through the intense study of Holy Scripture. Man cannot carry on this heavy combat if he does not know himself, the most important aspect of which is the recognition that spiritually he belongs to God, even if in the body, to the world. Erasmus then adds some twenty-two rules by which man must abide in order to obtain true happiness. Most of them he treats briefly, but in the fifth rule, the ascent from the visible to the invisible, he goes into great detail, as he does in the sixth rule, which portrays Christ as the ideal of piety. Some critiqued the work as tending towards Luther's rejection of good works (that is, an over-emphasis on the spiritual). Erasmus attacked monastic vows, distrusted ceremonies and sought to dismantle the entire external structure of medieval religion. We can see why it would be popular with the followers of Luther. Erasmus contrasts the spirit and the flesh, the spirit and the letter, light and darkness. External signs and ceremonies, he argues, are no longer necessary once the child in Christ has become a man. Rather than venerate the bones of St Paul, Erasmus says, honour the spirit that lives in his writings. Rather than venerate a fragment of the cross, it is better to listen to the words of Christ. To give two quotes:

> God is spirit, and he is moved by spiritual sacrifices…He is mind, the purest and the simplest of minds. Therefore he must be worshipped above all with a pure mind.

> Blessed…are they who hear the word of God within. Happy those to whom the Lord speaks inwardly, and their souls will be saved.[19]

It is from this evangelical freedom, and not from slavery to external commandments, that Erasmus expects everything. Erasmus saw himself as the true defender of the freedom of the Christian. The danger is that man is drawn away from Christ by the externals. Most priests, theologians and bishops, according to Erasmus, fall into this error.

In response to the call to define more dogma, Erasmus, rather, sets out the call to a holy life. And in a sense, once again, we can see here in the *Enchiridion* the tension we have been considering in the discussion of humanism. A spiritual, reforming agenda, resistance to the corruption of the church, yet also perhaps an overarching moralism, a quest for holiness, perhaps even excessive spiritualisation that goes some way to explaining why Erasmus did not follow Luther into Reform.

2. *Praise of Folly*

The origin of the book lay in Erasmus' return to England in 1509. He did not want to waste his time on idle gossip and was looking forward to seeing friends including Thomas More. More's name led Erasmus to the Latin, *moria*, which means foolishness or folly, and hence to the satirical *Praise of Folly*.

Part 1 has Folly ruling over humanity. Her father is money, her wet-nurses were Drunkenness and Ignorance, her maids of honour include Flattery, Idleness and Pleasure. With these faithful servants, everything in the world is under her sway. Erasmus asks, 'why are stupid people happy?'

> To begin with, these people have no fear of death…They are neither tortured by dread of impending disaster nor under the strain of hopes of future bliss. In short, they are untroubled by the thousand cares to which our life is subject.[20]

Folly also looks at religious practice.

> A man will soon become rich if he approaches Erasmus on the proper days with the proper bits of candle and the proper scraps of prayer.[21]

And as Augustijn comments:

> Indulgences, reciting particular prayers, the special patron saints of a given area, the specialized aid of saints – Appollonia for toothache, Hyacinth for the pangs

> of childbirth, Anthony for theft – it is all pointed out relentlessly.²²

The second part of the *Praise of Folly* turns to a traditional theme, criticism of the various classes and groups in society, from writers, teachers to, of course, monks, popes, cardinals and bishops! Few are spared Folly's caustic observations. When it comes to theologians, mockery yields to anger and rage. The bishops and clergy face the sharpest critique. The Popes, he says, seek glory in war, and through every rank of the church the harvest of money plays the chief role.

Part 3 puts these groups up against Scripture and are found wanting. In later editions, Erasmus explicitly introduces humanist characters, 'men of three tongues,' namely, Hebrew, Latin and Greek in contrast to the scholastic theologians.

In all, 36 editions of the Praise of Folly were printed and as Augustijn says, "the book offers an unsurpassed expression of the spirit of its author."²³

Erasmus' Greek edition of the New Testament

Erasmus believed that all education must have as its goal the training of readers to understand Scripture. Consequently, the consummate achievement of his life was his biblical translation and scholarship, most particularly his *Novum Testamentum*, his own edition of the New Testament. Here was the culmination of his humanist scholarship and methodology and it was here that Erasmus laid the egg that Luther hatched; an accurate, biblical text, derived from the original languages, which undermined so much of the structure of the medieval church which both Erasmus and Luther campaigned against and was laid bare against the analysis of an accurate Scriptural text.

Erasmus' work consisted of an edited version of the Greek New Testament, a Latin translation, and a set of annotations, these latter comprising a set of notes on the text to help the reader understand it. The Greek edition, put together from a compilation and comparison of as many of the oldest manuscripts Erasmus could find, allowed scholars to consult the original text. Hence they could evaluate Erasmus' conclusions by consulting the original text itself; classic humanism at work. The purpose of the Latin translation was to give readers an opportunity to see how careful scholarly assessment might lead to a different translation into Latin than the familiar Vulgate version.

Erasmus's New Testament went through five editions in his lifetime, in 1516, 1519, 1522, 1527 and 1535. Erasmus approached his work based on two principles:

1. The Vulgate version was corrupted leading to

misinterpretation
2. Linguistic use had changed and readers needed to understand the original meaning

Medieval western Christianity knew the Bible almost exclusively through the fourth-century Latin translation made by Jerome, known as the Vulgate (meaning, the common version). There were in fact several versions in circulation. Such was the importance that came to be attached to the Vulgate text that by the middle of the fourteenth century it appeared to have acquired an unchallengeable, almost divine status. There were, however, a number of problems and issues with the Vulgate:

- Copyists' errors in the several versions

There were, as manuscripts were originally copied by hand, inevitably errors which crept in during the process of copying. These was exposed when printed versions of the Vulgate began to be produced in the mid-fifteenth century, but this did not resolve which was the accurate version, although some of the more obvious errors were able to be corrected.

- The impact of glosses on the text

Perhaps of more long-term significance was the impact of the glosses. Essentially what happened as the text was copied was that comment was made upon the text in the margin, then comment upon comment and so on. In essence the meaning of the original text became disguised and meaning and interpretation came to be understood only through the medium of the glosses. In time, and as printed versions of text became available, these glosses were codified. The most significant was the *Glossa Ordinaria*, a work which had several authors and multiple sources and was in essence a continuous, composite and extended commentary on the

Bible and which acquired an authority equal to the text itself. As McGrath states:

> The essential point to appreciate here is that the contemporary reader of Scripture tended to approach the text of Scripture indirectly, through the interpretive gloss, encountering directly the accumulated wisdom of previous interpreters rather than the text itself. Errors on the part of enthusiastic copyists occasionally led to glosses being incorporated into the text of Scripture itself, leading to an unintended yet even more significant influence of the glossator upon the reader.[24]

- Mistranslations from the original languages

As the humanist scholars began to turn to original Hebrew and Greek manuscripts, Erasmus' Greek New Testament, with its new translation into Latin, exposed a number of very significant mistranslations which had carried forward into the Vulgate and which had deep importance for both church reform and Reformation doctrine. Here are two examples:
- Luke 1:2   'accepted into grace' rather than 'full of grace'
- Matthew 4:17   'be penitent' rather than 'do penance'

The implications are clear to see. The entire system of purgatory was built on the idea of 'doing penance' prescribed by the Church and hence receiving a remittance of sins, drawing on the Church's alleged reservoir of grace. The new translation exposed the sham. What Erasmus did was provide a new text in the original language based upon original manuscripts and then a translation into Latin which put the Vulgate version under new scrutiny. We can see how this fed into Luther's Reformation. When Erasmus published his New Testament, he wrote movingly and sincerely in its Prologue about his wish to see the countryman chant the Bible at his plough, the weaver at his loom, the traveller on his journey – even women should read the text. He wanted to end the excesses of clerical privilege, particularly the clergy's pretensions to special knowledge, and he was always ready to show contempt both for incompetent and unlearned clergy and for what he saw as the pompous obscurity of professional theologians. We should not underestimate in any way the significance of the humanist project in the publication by Erasmus of his *Novum Testamentum*.

Conclusion and evaluation

In conclusion, let me summarise, firstly, the significance of humanism for the Reformation. It saw a return to the original sources and an emphasis on the priority of the text. There was a concern for authenticity, clarity and truth, and great weight was given to the spiritual. Erasmus' Novum Testamentum had a central place. And the reforming nature of humanism carried through into the Reformation.

However, there were some areas of discontinuity. Humanism dealt with form rather than substance, reform rather than Reform. While it was spiritual, it was not doctrinal and was based on an over optimistic view of human nature, with too much emphasis on free will.

How does this all relate to modern humanism? Let me offer a few final thoughts. We have seen traces of the humanistic, individualist rationalism which eventually led to the rejection of God in the Enlightenment. Maybe when dealing with modern humanism we should:
- Constantly remind humanists of their Christian origins;
- Recall them to their original methods of original sources and priority of text;
- Give thanks for the quest for the spiritual and for reform;
- Hold firm to Christian doctrine and truth in Scripture as recovered in the Reformation.

Humanism, in its true, original Christian form was not the Reformation. It was, however, the means and the mechanism through which God, in large part, brought about the Reformation.

The return to the sources, the principles of clarity and accuracy came to fruition in the new Greek edition of the New Testament. God's Word was recovered in both purpose and clarity. The true Reformers took this crucial work and applied it to the failings of the medieval church, including doctrine and belief. Today we Christians benefit enormously from an appreciation of this heritage; thanks be to God for his Word.

References

1. Diarmaid MacCulloch, *Reformation: Europe's House Divided 1490-1700*, (London: Penguin, 2004), 81-82
2. Alister McGrath, *The Intellectual Origins of the European Reformation*. (London: Blackwell Publishing, second edition, 2004)
3. McGrath, *Intellectual Origins*, 35
4. MacCulloch, *Reformation*, 77
5. MacCulloch, *Reformation*, 81
6. Timothy George, *Theology of the Reformers*, (Nashville: Apollos, 1988), 47
7. Erasmus, *Praise of Folly,* quoted in George, *Theology,* 47
8. MacCulloch, *Reformation*, 81
9. MacCulloch, *Reformation*, 81
10. Richard Rex, 'Humanism', in Andrew Pettegree (ed), *The Reformation World*, (Abingdon: Routledge, 2000), 59
11. Rex, *'Humanism',* 59
12. McGrath, *Intellectual Origins*, 43
13. McGrath, *Intellectual Origins*, 48-49
14. McGrath, *Intellectual Origins*, 43
15. George, *Theology,* 49
16. J. Laurel Carrington, 'Desiderius Erasmus', in Carter Lindberg, *The Reformation Theologians*, (Oxford: Blackwell, 2002, 34)
17. Cornelius Augustijn, *Erasmus: His Life, Works and Influence*, (Toronto: University of Toronto Press, 2015), 22
18. Augustijn, *Erasmus*, 28
19. Augustijn, *Erasmus*, 48
20. Augustijn, *Erasmus*, 59
21. Augustijn, *Erasmus*, 59-60
22. Augustijn, *Erasmus*, 60
23. Augustijn, *Erasmus*, 69
24. McGrath, *Intellectual Origins*, 124